LEARNING THRU DISCUSSION

Guide for Leaders and Members of Discussion Groups

WM. FAWCETT HILL

Introduction by **HERBERT A. THELEN**

A SageMark Edition

SAGE PUBLICATIONS / BEVERLY HILLS ● LONDON

For information address:

SAGE PUBLICATIONS, INC.
275 South Beverly Drive
Beverly Hills, California 90212

SAGE PUBLICATIONS LTD
28 Banner Street
London EC1Y 8QE, England

Second revised edition

Printed in the United States of America

International Standard Book Number 0-8039-0711-7

Library of Congress Catalog Card No. 78-87064

FIFTH PRINTING, 1982

CONTENTS

ACKNOWLEDGMENTS

The material presented in this manual stems from two main sources. One source is a previous pamphlet published by the Center for the Study of Liberal Education for Adults in Chicago, Notes and Essays No. 22, entitled *Learning and Teaching Thru Discussion* and authored by Ida S. Hill and Wm. Fawcett Hill. Acknowledgment is made of their permission to reprint sections from this pamphlet, in which the rationale and educational philosophy underlying the discussion-group method was dealt with quite extensively. The present publication is more of a 'How To' manual. Therefore, thoughtful instructors contemplating using this method of learning through discussion would find it helpful to consult the original presentation. The other source is with the experience gained over the past ten years with the method. *LTD* has been used in a variety of settings, with a wide variety of professionals and para-professionals and in teaching a variety of subject matters. The cooperation of the student nurses at Utah State Hospital and the students in introductory psychology classes at Idaho State College with *LTD* is gratefully acknowledged. The difficulties encountered in the execution of the method led to a sharpening of the tools and the development of techniques of reinforcement which have helped in the maximizing of the potential of the method.

Contacts over the years with our colleagues in group development have had an influence apparent on every page, but in particular the impact of Jack Gibb and Hubert Coffey is mentioned. It was Dr. Ida S. Coppolino's appreciation of Coffey's concept of group cognitive map making that led to her original formulation of the method presented here. All of the psychologists at Utah State Hospital who were on the staff from 1956 to 1961 participated in the development and utilization of the method; particularly mentioned is the supervisory work of Richard Gross and Neil Sherwood.

Finally, gratitude is expressed to the many instructors who have continued to use *LTD*, especially Jerome Rabow, Alan Anderson, and Don Long. The confidence of such people has encouraged me to bring out this publication.

—*Wm. Fawcett Hill*

IN MEMORY OF

NORA J. GROSS

INTRODUCTION

HERBERT A. THELEN

Knowledge, we are told, can be learned for "ornamentation" or for "use"; as a possession which distinguishes middle class from lower class (let us say) or as "internalized" guidelines actually useful for intelligent, adaptive, or creative behavior. From the Depression to the present, the swing has been toward ornamentation, and the ornament most sought is a diploma or degree, which separates those who will be part of the productive society from those who won't. The diploma is gotten in exchange for a passel of lesser certificates and examinations—much like getting a toaster for several books of green stamps. The certificates or test results are not actually very ornamental—I certainly would not frame one to hang in the living room; but as psychic possessions they are counted and recounted, appraised and assayed, sources of hope or despair. The chief learning route for psychic ornamentation is memorization, enumeration, quotation, and standardization. One learns to say the "right" thing in each of the situations distinguishable by members of his social community. This performance in the *role* of "student" finds its most artistic expression in test wiseness; and education is operationally definable as learning how to respond to tests by listening to lectures on the same material and by studying the lecturer who usually doubles as the test maker.

This little book is *not* about knowledge for ornamentation, learning as collecting, or how to separate the sheep from the goats. This little book is about the process of acquiring knowledge for use. It is a modest book, untroubled by pretension. It knows its place and is supremely confident and secure in that knowledge—and can therefore be really helpful to those whose expectations are realistic. Perhaps the way I can be most useful is as a middleman, trying to show just where the book fits into typical concepts of the instructional sequence and what kinds of usefulness it has. Obviously, in *Learning Thru Discussion* it is assumed that there is something to be learned, and you don't have to get very far in the book before Dr. Hill speaks of learning materials that are to be studied by the student before the discussion begins.

Generally speaking, then, educators tend to think of sequences of activities, and each sequence has a beginning and end. (The "unit" plans made this very explicit.) Thus one can think of presentation (by the teacher), recitation (catechism), and testing, as a simpleminded sort of unit—and the reader would be astonished to learn how well this 1870 (or earlier) sequence fits most teaching in high schools today. Or, moving up to the twenties, he might find a sequence of overview (or stimulation), presentation, assimilation, application, and evaluation. Coming to the present, he would find a number of more sophisticated inquiry models (Taba, Suchman, Thelen, et al.) which gain in precision and elegance at the expense of generality.

Any adequate conception of *instructional* sequences has to somehow make room for the student alone with the materials; the student interacting with other students; the teacher intervening to focus activity and maintain its purposive, or means-ends, function. The part of the sequence that *Learning Thru Discussion* concerns itself with is the personal-social "interactive" (person-to-person, face-to-face) use of ideas presented in learning materials.

Any adequate conception of *curriculum* has to provide a rationale for the decisions which must be made before instruction can begin. How shall we decide what purposes to realize? How shall we select or create the materials of instruction? How shall we group the students into hardworking classes? And so on. Some educators would insist that *all* of these decisions (and many more) should be made before the class assembles, as, for example, in the use of programmed learning. There are other educators who feel that *none* of these decisions should be made in advance; that students must participate in making the decisions and that such participation is necessary to "meaningful" learning. Most modern educators, particularly witting or unwitting "systems" theorists, tend to make some decisions in advance and then build into instruction the means for modifying and elaborating the decisions as they go; that is, they would lay out the task in general terms and then rely on information gained as the work proceeds, in order to decide exactly how to intervene, how much effort to put into it, what aspirations are reasonable, how to accommodate individual differences, etc. This "systems" view underlies Hill's approach. Starting with the materials already decided upon, Hill shows the variety of ways in which the material can be pinched, punched, squeezed, kicked, and, ultimately, mastered. And he offers a plan for keeping the discussion on the beam—self-correcting, unambiguous, goal-directed; one not only learns, he also knows what he has learned and what he can use it for; and it is only thus that knowledge can transfer or universalize or transcend the immediate situation in which it was learned.

One objection to any planned sequence of steps is that while it probably makes sense (perhaps) for some—such as the teacher—it cannot make sense for all. It must therefore be discriminatory. There is, of course, something to this charge of unfairness. There are certain skills one requires for any operation (including independent study), and those who have these skills have an easier time (and may learn less) than those who do not have the skills. But the implication is not that demands for skills should be thrown out, but that the situation be such that persons can get the help they need to learn the skills as they need them (which is the best time), and that they not be punished for deficiencies. The group discussion, then, should incorporate its own procedures for self-improvement, for automatic accommodation between members and group demands. A situation is, in short, unfair if one cannot meet its prerequisites of skill. It is also unfair if rewards are unavailable to some, but not to others. Thus the second implication for Learning Thru Discussion is that a wide range of rewards be available so that there is something for everybody, some realistic point in striving. The range of rewards depends on the variety of things for which one can be rewarded, and Hill's scheme is unusually powerful in its explicit recognition of the great victory of task, group, and personal "roles" which are needed and which are therefore entitled to reward. The discussion sequence, with its variety of demands from step to step, is rich—rich in stimulation and rich in reward.

The idea of any plan or program for a group to be walked through annoys some people who like to emphasize spontaneity, individuality, creativity, permissiveness, humanity, etc.; and, by the same token, the idea of a plan or program for a group may have an unholy fascination for people who like to emphasize efficiency, predictability, security, orderly "development," etc. The *necessity* for a plan is not created by either attitude. It comes from the nature of groups themselves. One would need a general method, but not a stepwise plan, if he were working by himself. If he were working with two or three others, certain phases would probably be observed to form a sequence, but the chap himself might not be at all conscious of these phases. But when the group is larger *and* when it has a common purpose (which requires people to

listen to each other rather than merely to think out loud),
then there has to be enough definition of expectations so that
individuals know how to participate, can quite consciously
guide their own behavior, and can learn from the responses it
provokes in others. When two friends are chatting, they freely
and easily respond to whatever the other does—changes of
topic, mood, and feeling; but in a larger group, especially
when the members do not know each other (that is, do not
know what to expect from others), who is to say whether the
topic, mood, or feeling is to be changed? And who is to say
what the group should come up with, and whether the range
of ideas is adequate? One obvious answer, of course, is an
authoritarian leader—in which case the group spends its time
studying the leader. The other answer is clarity of purpose, in
which clarity is achieved both by having purposes immediately
recognizable as making sense and by taking the time to
rehearse quite concretely what is involved in satisfying each
(as, for instance, how much time to allow). The Hill scheme
substitutes methodological clarity for arbitrary leader authority, and it puts the leader in the role of helping the group
achieve its purposes rather than in the role of making
demands on the group and then (possibly hypocritically) add-
ing insult to injury by offering to help the group meet these
demands.

One further point in this overview: How literally or seriously or insistently is this formulation to be followed? Is it a
line-by-line recipe to be followed in all its exquisite detail?
Or is it an illustration of a few guidelines whose *application*
may differ markedly from one situation to the next? Or is it
a set of expectations of the sort of thing productive groups
do, so that no matter how the leader operates these expectations will be discernible within the system? One may, I think,
take it in all these ways. But I think there is a common
element underlying all the ways to use the formulation: it is a
conceptual model against which practice can be compared and

(hopefully) better penetrated and understood. I would suggest that one must face up to this model; if he want to modify it, leave out steps, place them in a different sequence, change the house rules—then he must explain to himself why; the burden of proof lies on him, not on the model. The beginner, I think, should literally touch all the bases in several sequences and, in the process, "internalize" the ideas of role, cooperation, function, control, etc. Then I think he will find himself beginning to make small variations, moving back and forth with previews and reviews even while following the main track. Ultimately a person might want to explicate his own ideas of some different logic of sequence and try them out; surely some differences would be expected depending on differences in the disciplines from which the learning materials come. Ideas, even as beautifully reasoned as Hill's, must finally free, not enslave, the teacher, and the features that finally remain as requirements are just those that ensure him the greatest scope for development of *his own* precious (and needed) abilities.

Professor Thelen is at the School of Education, University of Chicago.

THE ROLE OF LEARNING IN GROUP DISCUSSION

▨▨▨

EVER SINCE THE American Revolution the democratic way of life has been endorsed as the American way of life. Except for the electoral system, democracy as a way of life has in reality been resisted and for a very simple reason—it challenges the position of the vested authorities. There is a modern revolution which has gained great impetus in the last two decades and is characterized by the actual utilization of democratic concepts in many fields of human endeavor rather than confining them exclusively to the polling booth. It is termed a revolution because, as a social development, it is relatively rapid (although long heralded and long honored in the breach) and because it represents a partial overthrow of the traditional authority of such figures as the teacher, the therapist, the boss or owner, and the parent. The revolution has been carried out through the development of group work, which involves the recognition and utilization of the properties and potentials of the small face-to-face group. For a society to be truly democratic, it must in some way extend democratic principles to this fundamental social unit—the primary group. The evidence for asserting that such a revolution exists is partially provided by the phenomenal growth of participation in discussion groups, psychotherapy groups, conference groups, workshop groups and social group work as well as the rapid development in the science of group dynamics.

As in all revolutions, there are abuses carried on in the name of democracy, and this is certainly true in the democratizing of the classroom. The discussion group, which is the topic of this article, has been the principal influence in introducing democratic principles into the educational process, and in so doing has undoubtedly been guilty of abuses and excesses. Because of this, and also because it does challenge the authority of the teacher, it is hardly surprising that there is much criticism directed at the discussion-group approach. Much of it can be readily turned against the critics and the traditional position they apparently defend. We prefer to take the criticism seriously rather than deflect it, even though we are obviously biased toward the group approach. The reason for this stems from the fact that we are uneasy about current practices in group discussion. When the destructive criticism is absent, and the arguments against group discussion reduced to a common denominator, the salient objection of the critics is that the discussion group seriously vitiates the contribution of the highly trained and well-informed instructor. When the destructive criticism is present, the discussion group is often referred to as a case of 'the blind leading the blind,' or as an instance of people coming together to pool their ignorance.

Analysis of studies of discussion groups indicates that the discussion-group method did not emerge as superior in terms of academic achievement, interest in the course, increased skill in subject matter and so forth. On the other hand, it was not found to be inferior. Our review of these studies did supply the clue which led us to reexamine our assumptions about discussion in the classroom. The clue lay in the words used to describe the discussion method employed in the experimental settings—words like *unstructured, permissive, uncontrolled,* and *student-centered.* These words—all of which sound reminiscent of the Dewey-eyed educators of an earlier era and, which like them, are a reaction to authoritarian methods—may be emphasizing the pleasure principle at the expense of the reality principle, and confounding laissez faire with demo-cratic principles. If discussion groups are run along lines more appropriate to therapy groups, the validity of the foregoing criticism must be recognized and dealt with. Before dealing with the apparent weaknesses in the discussion-group approach, it is nonetheless remarkable that so much success has been claimed for this method by those who admittedly run groups under unstructured and often unsupervised condi-tions. There are in the literature many testimonials, sometimes backed up by student evaluations and by grades achieved, which contrast favorably with control groups. These testi-monials claim, in addition to comparable results in terms of performance on examinations, superiority in the significant areas of student involvement and enthusiasm for learning and even in the area of personality development. The sheer weight of testimony for the discussion-group approach is almost over-whelming. There seems to be little doubt that the discussion group will usually produce more personalized emotional effects of an educationally desirable nature, and we will not dwell on this point further.

Nevertheless, we are not completely overwhelmed and cannot help noticing that the majority of teaching is done by the tra-ditional methods and in fact, many of the advocates of the discussion group desert the method any time that subject matter of any degree of difficulty must be thoroughly mastered. In short, the discussion method is usually reserved for such courses as Marriage and the Modern Family, Understanding Modern Art, or Citizenship. Even the critics agree that the dis-cussion group is good if the goal is attitude formation or opinion-sharing. The question that is of concern in this pam-phlet is whether group discussion can be used effectively to meet stringent requirements of subject matter mastery. The position taken here is that mastery of difficult material can be achieved through the discussion group, but not with permissive and unstructured approaches.

The main point that we would like to make is that in using the discussion-group approach the teacher is involved in *group work* as well as in the content of the course. If the group is to be used as an educational device, which is presumably the rationale for not lecturing in the first place, then the instructor needs to have some knowledge of group process, group development, and group dynamics. Most instructors who 'have tried it and didn't like it' did not have any sophistication in group techniques; failure and frustration could have readily been anticipated. One principle of group work at issue here is that, for a group to achieve its objectives, the members need to have some understanding of the roles they must execute. The typical student in our culture has had little preparation for participation in a discussion group as his academic experience has been dominated by lecture methods. Thus the students and the group flounder and turn to the instructor for help. Due to the instructor's own lack of understanding of group work, or his allegiance to permissiveness, he usually cannot or will not provide the training necessary for a productive learning group. A partial remedy for this situation would be for the leader to consult one of the many excellent discussion leader guides that are available. However, excellent as they may be, they are more concerned with how to lead a lively discussion than with accomplishing the learning task. This pamphlet was prepared to provide for this need on the part of leaders or group members. This guide is not intended to supplant, but to supplement, other guides for discussion-group leaders.

As might already have been anticipated, we advocate, where didactic material must be mastered, that the discussion group have some method of proceeding. It must have a plan, a map, a program, or some agreed-upon procedure, and the idea that any random comment is appropriate grist for the mill is firmly rejected. Something other than free association by the whole group or domination by one member is indicated. Even if a student agrees that these things are not desirable, he nonetheless does not know how to proceed, and if he has some idea, it is in all likelihood not congruent with anyone else's. Thus the group is usually paralyzed and cannot take any productive steps forward. The instructor should have and should communicate some method for the group to carry on the discussion of the assigned topic.

Our analysis of studies of discussion groups also revealed that the discussion group was treated as an avant garde phenomenon. Obviously, discussion dates back at least to Socrates' time. The seminar was well established in the college curriculum long before there was widespread interest in the discussion method. However, a look at the typical seminar may be instructive.

Usually there is a requirement that each member present on some aspect of the course. Members therefore tend to focus their attention and energies on the area in which they are to present. Consequently, they tend to listen selectively to the presentations of others with the hope that they can shine in the group by diverting the discussion to their own area of expertise. At the conclusion of a presentation, it is not uncommon to hear a response that goes something like this: 'That was a quite adequate presentation, however, I feel that more might have been said about X.' X is of course the respondent's assigned area. This is recognized immediately by the reader as Seminarmanship. This particular ploy accomplishes two objectives in the one statement: namely, puts the presenter down, gently of course, and diverts the discussion to the area where the respondent can shine. Other Seminarmanship lore worth mentioning is the role of maintaining the status quo. If anyone in the group seems to be in need of help, either ignore his cry for assistance or throw him an anchor. After all, someone has to get the C's and D's, and once a member's ignorance has been exposed, it is best to let the chips (or grades) fall where they may. A corollary of this is never to indicate to the instructor that you have learned anything from the group discussion—again, this might rebound against you. There are other ploys too numerous to mention relating to how to be one up in a seminar, but the brief coverage here may suffice to indicate the grave insufficiency of the typical seminar as a vehicle for learning.

Before dealing with *LTD,* let us first examine the relationship between the student and the learning process, with a view towards discovering the requirements that a discussion group must meet to provide learning for the student. A student learns and passes his examinations by doing homework and class work. Usually the former requires silent studying of the text, and the latter involves attending lectures. In Learning Thru Discussion *(LTD)* the student must do his homework, which means reading the assignment. This cannot be postponed to the night before the examination but must be done prior to each and every group discussion period. Admittedly, discussion can go on without preparation, and, in fact, ignorance of the topic facilitates the development of heated discussions. The only trouble is that there is more heat generated than light.

Preparation for discussion in *LTD* makes special homework demands and will be covered in detail later in this manual.

How one learns about a subject in the lecture situation is self-evident, but how anyone learns in the discussion situation is a bit of a mystery to most students. A logical analysis of a group where the students come prepared reveals four possible conditions in which a student could find himself.

First of all, a student may have prepared his assignment and had no trouble understanding a particular topic. This we will call condition A. On the other hand, a student might not understand a particular topic—condition B. In the discussion group, it might happen that for a particular topic condition A prevails, i.e., everyone understands it. Groups often dwell at length on topics which everyone understands and they 'beat it to death.' The security operation is of course dominant and no learning takes place. The *LTD* method suggests, as we shall see, that the group bypass topics in which condition A prevails. Similarly, it may happen that condition B is prevalent and no one understands the topic. This does not necessarily inhibit discussion, and in fact, some of the most animated interaction takes place when no one knows what he is talking about. Again, however, no learning is taking place. The *LTD* method suggests that under this circumstance the resource expert or the text be consulted or, failing, this, the group move on. The above recommendations for conditions A and B indicate how learning groups can be efficient.

Usually, in a group, a mixed condition obtains. We do not have all A's or all B's but some of each. This is the true learning situation, and, for learning to take place, it is necessary for those who don't understand (B) to communicate this; and for those who do understand (A) to respond in kind. For different topics we would expect different people in the groups to occupy the A and B roles.

When this interaction prescription is in operation, we can see how information is shared and knowledge is disseminated throughout the group. It is clear how the B's have benefited— but how about the A's? When the A's and B's interact, two new categories emerge. Everyone has had the experience of trying to explain something to another person and realizing that his understanding is incomplete, hence condition C—not fully understanding that which you think you understand. This is perhaps the most crucial aspect for learning in the discussion group. In the group situation, it is possible to play the teaching role and as the old saying goes, you never really learn a subject until you teach it. Quite possibly one of the strengths of the old-fashioned one-room school house was that it was necessary that students in higher grades assist in the instruction of the children in the lower grades. There has been much current emphasis by Thelen and others on placing students in teaching roles as part of their educational development.

To complete the logical analysis, there is a fourth circumstance emerging from the interaction of so-called A's and B's— namely, when a person thinks he doesn't understand a topic but in reality does—condition D. It occurs when someone explains what it is he doesn't understand, and in formulating the question perceives the answer. (This is sometimes called thinking out loud.)

Thus, we have learning taking place, according to this formal analysis, through the interaction of the A's and B's and the generating of two new types—C's and D's. It is not too difficult, therefore, to see, structurally, the potential for learning that exists in a group.

However, students often have great verbal facility and can drop names and facts with the greatest of ease and yet not have real understanding of the basic concepts. The logical analysis offered above does not deal with pseudo-learning, and *LTD,* while it does take advantage of the group potential, also introduces procedures to minimize the so-called pseudo-learning that abounds in education. In particular, the Group Cognitive Map, to be discussed in the next chapter, places strong emphasis on learning exactly what the author has to say on a subject.

Another advantage of this method is that in helping each other, the students, are communicating at about the same level, whereas the instructor may be going over their heads. Also, students often have the frustrating experience of not understanding some aspect of the course and being unable to state the source of their difficulty. Other students who approach the material from the same disadvantage point can often diagnose the nature of a fellow student's difficulty much better than the instructor.

In the development of the *LTD* method, two considerations were uppermost; an appreciation of the method requires an understanding of the operation of these two fundamental conceptions. First, it must be kept in mind that a discussion group is a group and is, therefore, subject to the canons of group development and group dynamics. This obvious fact has apparently been overlooked by the didactically oriented discussion leader. Group interaction inevitably generates communication problems but it also exposes new potentials for learning; a method of group discussion should try to minimize the effect of these problems and maximize the group potential. Second, it must be kept in mind that this group-oriented consideration must not obscure the particular purpose of subject matter mastery. This obvious fact has apparently been overlooked by the group-oriented discussion leader. His goal is the development of a 'good' group, and the learning of the lesson becomes almost incidental. In such cases the definition of a good group is vague, high-sounding, and indisputable. It is indisputable because it is idealistic and untestable. If we pursue the considerations underlying the method, then a good group can be defined in more specific terms. A good group is one where the process, or communication, problems are adequately handled and the potential of the members realized, so that the learning of the course material is enhanced. *LTD* is designed to encompass the foregoing considerations, and the method consists of three parts: the Group Cognitive Map, Group Roles and Member Skills, and the List of Criteria. These are interrelated but must, perforce, be dealt with individually.

GROUP COGNITIVE MAP

AS HAS ALREADY been indicated, group discussions are often characterized by lack of direction, and the topics that are discussed arise fortuitously or at the insistence of a dominating member with the compliance of submissive, indifferent, or confused members. No one knows what behavior is appropriate to the situation or, if they think they do, they cannot be sure that anyone else would agree with them. Appropriate behavior actually consists of developing some procedure for adequately discussing the material. A poor plan that is endorsed and followed by all the members is better than none at all. Certainly, what is desirable is a program that logically relates to the goal of learning. The Group Cognitive Map is a procedural tool which outlines an orderly sequence that a group should follow in order to learn from discussion. It is the instructor's job to present this map to the group and to explain its significance and operation. For the Group Cognitive Map to be effective, a mandate must be derived from the group so that it can be put into operation with the consent and active support of the members. Once this is accomplished the group has a *shared* and agreed-upon method of proceeding. For a great many reasons, there will be both overt and covert resistance to accepting the Group Cognitive Map. The instructor must assert his prerogative to conduct the discussion group along the lines he thinks best.

The Group Cognitive Map is made up of nine steps which are presented here in tabular form. The rationale and behavior for each step will be dealt with in detail immediately following the tabulation. We assume the existence of suitable study materials, available to all, and read prior to the meeting.

GROUP COGNITIVE MAP

Step One	–	Definition of terms and concepts
Step Two	–	General statement of author's message
Step Three	–	Identification of major themes or sub-topics
Step Four	–	Allocation of time
Step Five	–	Discussion of major themes and subtopics
Step Six	–	Integration of material with other knowledge
Step Seven	–	Application of the material
Step Eight	–	Evaluation of author's presentation
Step Nine	–	Evaluation of group and individual performance

Step One — Definition of Terms and Concepts

One objective of the Group Cognitive Map is to lessen the possibility of the group's becoming involved in useless argument. It is now standard operating procedure to define terms before discussing any subject. This avoids the so-called semantic trap which ensnares so many groups. Also, the act of defining terms in itself constitutes learning. In introductory courses, mastering the technical language is often half the course, and where objective tests are used, covers half the examination. Consequently, in some courses considerable time might legitimately be spent on this step. One pitfall is the tendency for a student to extend the definition of a term into a resume of the whole assignment. The instructor will probably have to indicate what is appropriate for this step. In reading technical and scientific material, it is often necessary to consult dictionaries specific to the field under consideration. Most students have to be told that Webster's is not infallible and that for certain terms it can be either unrewarding or misleading. Often the instructor has to make such technical and scientific dictionaries available.

Step Two — General Statement of Author's Message

The purpose of this step is to obtain some grasp of the overall meaning of the assigned reading. Enunciation of a general statement should accomplish this. It also demarcates the area to be discussed, that is, it zeros in on the topic for discussion. It also serves the purpose of launching the discussion. Some authors, particularly of textbooks, begin each chapter with a clearly designated general statement which greatly simplifies the student's task and thereby lessens the time spent in this step. Even so, the members should state the general purpose of the assignment in their own words. Quite often the task is not so simple, and the determination of the author's main point is no small intellectual accomplishment. In these circumstances the formulation of the author's overall message may in itself constitute important learning and may also greatly facilitate the task to be encountered in Step Three.

Step Three — Identification of Major Themes or Subtopics

Most material can be broken down into a number of important subtopics. Again, authors of textbooks not only organize their material in this fashion but even provide subheadings. Although most of the job is thereby done for the student, these subtopics should be restated in the student's own words to assure his understanding. In other cases, a close analysis of the material is required to isolate and enunciate the subtopics, and usually much is learned in the pursuit of this task. It should be apparent that in *LTD* great emphasis is placed on determining what the author has to say, rather than on the opinions of the students.

Step Four — Allocation of Time

This is a crucial step in the method. The common complaint of discussion-group members is that they never cover the material and spend too much time on one aspect to the neglect of all the rest. To meet this real difficulty the group must budget its time, and conduct the discussion accordingly. Actually, there is never enough time in a group any more than there is in life, to accomplish everything, no matter how well budgeted the available time may be. This is particularly true in this case, when one considers that time must be made available, not only for the topics isolated in Step Three, but also to fulfill the requirements of Steps Five, Six, Seven, Eight, and Nine. The value of Step Four lies in the fact that the group sets its own time limits and, as a group, gains some grasp of the area to be discussed and can thereby regulate itself accordingly. The results obtained by omitting this step are not hard to visualize; in fact all readers have had unfortunate experiences with groups that had no regulatory clock and could not pace themselves appropriately. While this step is crucial, it is also the most difficult one of all for the groups to master. There are many obvious reasons for this. One invalid type of reasoning is, 'Since there is little enough time as it is, why use some of it up deciding about how much time is to be spent on each topic?' This would be valid if a group were heroically attempting to cover all the material. In the *LTD* method this is considered wasteful, and the discussion period should be used to deal with only those parts of the material that the members, for one reason or another, feel it would be most profitable to discuss. Usually some of the assigned reading is readily understood and need not be recapitulated. Learning to exercise this selectivity is not easy, and, at the outset, groups have difficulty in determining, with any degree of confidence, what needs and does not need discussion. Sometimes, the least understood parts are nominated for exclusion in order to avoid the embarrassment of exposing ignorance, and a group will prefer to discuss that which is already known. Also, the group cannot estimate accurately how much time is needed in Steps Five, Six, Seven, Eight, and Nine until it has had some experience with the method. The instructor must be prepared for the group's having difficulty with this step and encourage it to persevere.

Step Five — Discussion of Major Themes and Subtopics

It is important to note that so far in the *LTD* method there has been no acutal discussion of the assignment, only a clearing away and tooling up for the discussion! The discussion should proceed within the strictures laid down in Step Four, wherein the topics have been selected and time and priority have been allocated. As might be anticipated, groups will become frustrated with their inability to carry out their own decisions in regard to allocation of time, and this will negatively affect the quality of the discussion. What is to be done in this step is clear, but it is more easily explained than executed. The *LTD* method does not create these problems; it only makes the group aware of them.

In this step, as in Steps Two and Three, the emphasis is still on the author's message and not on the personal opinions of the group members. As has been emphasized, any expression of the personal reactions of members has so far been forbidden by the method. This is not because these are thought to be of no significance. Quite the contrary, it is only that we have found in our experience that groups never discover what the author has to say if they begin by giving their personal opinions. Inevitably this leads to diversions or disagreement. Sides are drawn up, and what the author has to say becomes of only incidental importance. Thus, in *LTD* the expression of personal reactions is postponed until the group has discussed the text. The idea of being acquainted with what authorities in a field actually say is, in itself, a novel development in many discussion circles. For example, most people have very decided opinions on evolution, psychoanalysis, and communism and yet have read little or nothing by Darwin, Freud, or Marx. *LTD* is intended to counteract this condition, but the instructor will find resistance to a method which curbs the members' self-expression. He must try to get the group members to channel these personal observations into Step Eight. This requires delay of gratification, which is usually considered a mark of maturity, and therefore cannot be expected to be readily practiced early in the life of a group. The demand for self-expression and the inability of the group to complete the discussion of a topic within the alloted time will be the two main problems encountered in this step.

Step Six — Integration of Material with Other Knowledge

An oft-heard criticism of the educational system is that learning is too fragmentary and too much concerned with the acquisition of isolated bits of information. The use of multiple choice and true-false examinations reinforces this kind of learning. It is a well-known fact of learning theory that isolated, unassociated facts are the first to be forgotten. Even if they are retained, they may still be unattached to any body of knowledge and are therefore of limited value.

To counteract this possibility, *LTD* requires group members to allocate time and make a conscious effort to relate learnings in the assignment to ideas and concepts acquired in previous meetings or other learning situations. If this is carried out successfully, over a period of time a student should amass a body of knowledge that would be more integrated and more likely to be retained.

Again, we may find that in introductory courses the student feels he does not have much to interrelate. As the course proceeds, this step may come to have a more important function. In some advanced courses this may well be the most vital of all the steps, and proportionately more time would be devoted to it. At the outset, an instructor may have to provide examples of cross-referencing and integrating in order for the student to grasp the cognitive task appropriate to this step.

Step Seven -- Application of the Material

The criticism of the educational system raised above occurs again here in a slightly altered form. Knowledge should not only be accumulative and integrated, but it also should have personal value or significance for the student. Subject matter mastery should enhance feelings of ego mastery. Acquired knowledge that is not internalized and remains ego-alien is either readily forgotten, or results in the creation of arid scholasticism or mere pedantry. The reader is invited to conjecture on the extent to which learning in our schools and colleges is unintegrated and meaningless to the student.

To counteract this likelihood, *LTD* requires group members to allocate time and make a conscious effort to assess the possible applications and implications of the material. Some subjects, e.g., psychology, often have very direct personal application. Others may have less personal application, but many implications of an intellectual nature that the student can develop. Again, in introductory courses the students usually have difficulty in seeing the relevance of the lesson, and the instructor, may at the outset have to provide the group with appropriate examples.

Step Eight — Evaluation of the Author's Presentation

At long last, the personal reactions of the student are programmed into the method. The rationale for this postponement has already been given. In addition, it is often the case that after covering the other steps, the students' criticism has less affective loading and becomes more constructive. From group-work theory, we know that affective reactions will out, and the method should not be used to squelch them, but only to provide an appropriate time and place for their expression and also, hopefully, to encourage their outlet in a more goal-directed and sublimated form. A particularly turgid piece of writing can be very frustrating, and the student has every right to give vent to his feelings of frustration. If learning is to be served, however, criticism should become critique and, rather than being eliminated, should be raised to a level of incisiveness. The development of the ability to think critically may well be more important than the learning of the material itself, as it will serve the student well in all future learning and life situations. Consequently, if this step can be something in addition to affective unloading, namely the development of the critical faculty, this may well be the greatest accomplishment of the method.

The development of the ability to evaluate reading assign-
ments does not come as easily as the rendering of affective
reactions, and students usually will require from the instructor
many examples before they feel competent to perform this
task.

Step Nine — Evaluation of Group and Individual Performance

For the method to work, this step is essential. As a matter
of fact, for any group to be effective some time must be
devoted to evaluating the inevitable individual problems and
group process problems. In the *LTD* method it is suggested
that approximately the last ten minutes of the hour be
devoted to diagnosing and evaluating the group and individual
effectiveness. Many well-trained group leaders would insist on
dealing with group problems as they are manifested, rather
than handling them at a specific time. That they *are* handled
is more important than *when* they are handled. Both on-the-
spot and scheduled approaches have been used without any
evidence indicating which one is better. The only point that
can be made is that the logic of the method suggests that
evaluation should be set aside as a separate step and that the
group budget time for it. On-the-spot inquiries have the
advantage of immediacy, but also have the disadvantage of
preventing the group from staying within its self-imposed time
budget, thereby providing an alibi for its shortcomings. A
group will invariably find difficulty in utilizing the Group
Cognitive Map when it is starting out, and it should be forced
to face up to this and overcome it. Otherwise the method will
always be frustrating and self-defeating.

As this step is so important and also so specialized, it will
be dealt with separately and at some length after the Group
Cognitive Map, Group Roles and Member Skills, and the List
of Criteria have been covered. At this point it can be men-

tioned that while the analysis of individual role and group process problems is highly specialized, the *LTD* method is designed to greatly simplify the task. Again, the instructor can be helpful by example, sharing his diagnosis, insights, and interpretations of what is occurring in this group. This will give the group members a model to follow. This, too, will be dealt with more fully in a section covering the responsibilities of the instructor.

All groups generate both individual and group problems and the added requirement of mastering the Group Cognitive Map makes it necessary that time be devoted to this step. As a group develops, however, it should not need to compulsively go through the motions expected in Step Nine, but only use it from time to time as needed.

A final word on the Group Cognitive Map. The technique should be used appropriately and creatively, which means that the allotment of time to the steps should vary for different groups, subjects, and course goals. The disbursement of the sequence of steps may be varied for a particular group as it develops. Furthermore, the steps may be altered to meet idiosyncratic conditions, and the Group Cognitive Map reported here is intended more as a general plan and guide for the instructor or group member. The instructor should assess the nature of the material, his course objectives, the kind of student he will be dealing with and formulate his own version of the Group Cognitive Map, before the group meets.

The term 'group cognitive map,' was introduced by Coffey in programming a logical sequence of steps for problem-solving groups. The term 'cognitive map' was borrowed from Tolman, who used it in his learning theories to explain the behavior of rats running mazes. Learning to use the Group Cognitive Map may invite an unflattering parallel with learning to run a maze. The parallel diverges only when there is added to this structure the function of the other two parts of the *LTD* method—the Group Roles and Member Skills, and the List of Criteria.

GROUP ROLES AND MEMBER SKILLS

EARLIER, IT WAS STATED that for a discussion to be successful there must be recognition that it is truly a *group* situation, and principles of group work should apply. One important principle is that certain roles have to be performed and members must have the interpersonal skill to perform them. Ever since K. D. Benne's and P. Sheats's original article on group roles ('Functional Roles of Group Members,' *Journal of Social Issues,* vol. 4 no. 2, 1948), workshops and laboratories in human relations training have been developing lists of group roles. No complete or final list can be prepared, and the one presented here is not exhaustive but selective. The selection has been guided by the learning theory implicit in *LTD* as well as by group theory.

Group roles are usually classified as 'group maintenance,' or 'task accomplishment,' or both. This distinction is observed in our organization of group roles. In it we have followed the standard nomenclature found in group-work literature. Usually there is much overlap and repetition, and this has been deliberately minimized by grouping the overlapping roles into three functional clusters:

    A. Sequence of task roles specific to discussion of a topic,
    B. Overall task roles required in the *LTD* method,
    C. Group maintenance roles required in the *LTD* method.

Before presenting in tabular form the list of roles and a detailed description of each, a few words of caution about role theory is indicated. Group roles, in amended form, were previously leader roles; with the democratization of the group, members must assume the responsibilities that leaders were presumed to carry out. In the assumption of this responsibility it is best not to have a simple division of labor with one role for each member. An effective group member can and should perform many, if not all, the group roles with some finesse. A member playing any one role consistently and persistently will be more of a hindrance than a help. There is a concept of appropriateness inherent in the exercise of group roles and a need for member sensitivity is indicated.

GROUP ROLES AND MEMBER SKILLS

A. Sequence of task roles specific to discussion of a topic

1. Initiating
2. Giving and asking for information
3. Giving and asking for reactions
4. Restating and giving examples
5. Confronting and reality testing
6. Clarifying, synthesizing, and summarizing

B. Overall task roles required in the *Learning Thru Discussion* method

7. Gatekeeping and expediting
8. Timekeeping
9. Evaluating and diagnosing
10. Standard setting

C. Group maintenance roles required in the *Learning Thru Discussion* method

11. Sponsoring and encouraging
12. Group tension relieving

A. Sequence of Task Roles Specific to Discussion of a Topic

1. *Initiating.* Sometimes a group has trouble getting started or resuming discussion when a lull falls upon it. Apparently each member is waiting for someone else to get the group going. Anyone *can* break the sound barrier, but someone *must.* The basis for reluctance to perform this routine service, like the resistance to performing any task or maintenance role, often lies in a member's unwillingness to be perceived and thereby rejected as an aspiring leader. Resistance to getting down to work is also commonly found in the performance of these roles.

2. *Giving and asking for information.* In the *LTD* method, students are required to state the general message and the ideas contained in the subtopics. In a well-developed group this information will be readily volunteered, but in beginning groups it may have to be solicited. The members must share their understandings of the material freely or else the discussion will be awkward and stilted.

3. *Giving and asking for reactions.* When a member does share his understanding of a point, groups often treat it as a curtain closer and remain silent or move on without comment. For learning to take place some reaction should be volunteered or solicited. In some groups there is no interaction; instead there is a rotation process, and one member states his understanding of a topic and passes it on to the member on his right who gives his understanding on the next topic and so on. This type of group ritual results in little learning since no one is listening, but reciting to himself the offering he will render when it comes around to his turn. Usually, but not always, explanations by one member merit or could be enhanced by reactions from others. If there is no feedback, the members are not going to get much more out of the discussion than they could obtain from silent reading.

4. *Restating and giving examples.* This is usually a specific type of 3, giving and asking for reactions. If a member restates what another has said, he provides feedback to the original speaker. By restating he provides a test of whether the member accurately communicated what he intended. The value of giving examples cannot be overemphasized. A good example illuminates for all the meaning of what is being said in a way that no amount of elaboration can accomplish.

5. *Confronting and reality testing.* This is involved in 3, giving and asking for reactions and 4, restating and giving examples. Certainly one form of reality testing is to restate in your own words what someone else has just said. This provides a test of communication and of the correctness of the idea in the message. Many groups allow misinformation and misstatements to pass by. Allegedly, this is done in order not to embarrass the speaker; actually it is to save themselves embarrassment. Confronting is an important function if learning is to take place. Suggesting that someone else's statement is not entirely accurate requires skill and ego strength.

6. *Clarifying, synthesizing, and summarizing.* Even with the simplest of material, groups can get into complicated tangles and are, from time to time, in great need of someone to play the clarifying role. Also, where a number of restatements of a topic have been made, for example, synthesis is needed. Clarifying and synthesizing have the value of providing closure, as does summarizing, and allowing the group to move on to the next item on the agenda.

B. Overall Task Roles Required in *Learning Thru Discussion*

7. *Gatekeeping and expediting.* One of the most common behaviors in fulfilling this role involves attempts to spread

participation. A typical gatekeeping remark is, "We haven't heard from X; what do you think about . . . ?" Gatekeeping, or expediting, is directly connected with holding the group to the Group Cognitive Map and moving it through its steps.

8. *Timekeeping.* This is a specific instance of 7, gatekeeping and expediting, and is of particular importance in the *LTD* method. If a group is to keep within its time budget, someone must keep an eye on the clock, at least until the group learns to pace itself automatically. It is desirable for members to become involved, but this often means neglect of the budgeted time for a topic, and if this role is neglected, the group may not pass through all the phases of the discussion.

9. *Evaluating and diagnosing.* In the Group Cognitive Map, evaluation and diagnosis is deferred until Step Nine, and then it is expected that most, if not all, will participate. Even when this procedure is adhered to, members need to silently fill this role during the ongoing discussion or else there will be little to bring up when Step Nine is reached. One technique that has been successfully used is to assign one member to be the process observer, and he makes a report, at Step Nine, of the observations he has garnered throughout the discussion. Some training and experience is required to fulfill this role, but checking against the requirements of the Group Cognitive Map, Group Roles and Member Skills, and the List of Criteria (to be discussed in the next section) is sufficient for understanding most group problems.

10. *Standard setting.* This is sometimes called the group's 'ego ideal,' and the role requirement is to indicate to the group the standards of performance that they have implicitly or explicitly set for themselves. This role should be activated when there is a wide discrepancy between current performance and group standards. The next section, the List of

Criteria, sets forth explicitly the standards required by the *LTD* method; operation in this role will be more readily understood if this section is consulted. *LTD* suggests that this role and 9, evaluating and diagnosing, be exercised in Step Nine of the Group Cognitive Map, but, as stated earlier, there is no evidence at this time to indicate that on-the-spot use of these roles is contraindicated.

11. *Sponsoring and encouraging.* Roles 1, initiating, and 7, gatekeeping and expediting, are specific examples. Certain members need sponsoring from time to time and all members need encouragement. The encouraging remark is not only important to the recipient, but it also tends to contribute to a warm and accepting climate which in turn encourages voluntary participation. The giving of praise or encouragement seems to be alien to our culture. Because of this, students need encouragement in performing the encouraging role. Skill, as well as ego strength, is required in drawing out silent members. Inept performance of this role can have the opposite effect of that intended and can entrench a member in this nonparticipant behavior.

12. *Group tension relieving.* A role that might be likened to a thermostat should be available to be activated when tensions get too high. When discussions become deadly serious, or frustration over following the Group Cognitive Map becomes unbearable, or disagreements about the meaning of the material become intense, the thermostat should activate this tension-relieving role. Behaviors associated with the role are kidding, telling jokes, and making diverting and off-target remarks. Sometimes this role is referred to in the literature as harmonizing. It is worth noting that behaviors associated with this role are considered to be nonfunctional and disruptive when they are not in the service of group maintenance.

In the treatment of this topic, the nonfunctional roles are usually described in detail. While they are disruptive to the goals of the *LTD* method, there is nothing of a special quality introduced by the method. They are therefore listed without comment. If the reader does not find the roles to be self-evident from their titles, he can consult Benne and Sheats for further elucidation.

NONFUNCTIONAL ROLES

1. Aggressing
2. Blocking
3. Self-confessing
4. Competing
5. Seeking sympathy
6. Special interest pleader
7. Horsing around (playboy)
8. Status seeking
9. Withdrawing
10. Dominating

One role not included in the regular list of Group Roles and of particular importance in the *LTD* method is listening. The magazine supplements of the Sunday newspapers invariably have an article on the importance of being a good listener. Apparently if this role is completely mastered, all your ambitions will be realized. Our claims are more modest. Good listening will promote good interaction and learning. The distinction to be made is between active and passive listening. If members are actively listening their chances of learning something are greatly improved. If their 'hearing aid' is turned down, not only will they not learn anything, but they will have a very depressing effect on the participating members.

The significance of Group Roles should now be apparent. If many of these roles are missing from the discussion, it will inevitably bog down, and the learning potential of the discussion group will not be realized.

LIST OF CRITERIA
FOR A GOOD GROUP

〰〰〰〰〰〰〰〰〰〰〰〰〰〰〰〰〰〰〰〰〰〰〰〰〰〰〰〰〰〰〰

A NUMBER OF PROBLEMS connected with the use of the discussion group have been propounded. Perhaps, as with your Friendly Finance Company, all of these problems can be consolidated into one big problem! The overall problem is the inexperience of the typical student with the discussion method. The typical student, because of years of academic exposure, knows all too well what is expected of him and what he can expect from the traditional lecture situation. He has no similar set of expectations when confronted with the group discussion approach. This problem is compounded by the fact that not only is his previous academic experience of little help, but also his other experiences with formal groups have in all probability not been too satisfying. Thus even the most highly motivated student has difficulty being effective, because he has no model of a good group nor a clear image of the kind of behavior that would contribute to building one. Consequently, what is needed is a concept of what a good group should be, and this concept should be shared by all the group members. Goal-directed behavior cannot be achieved in the absence of shared goals.

The instructor's task therefore would be to help the group members to formulate some concept of what constitutes a good group learning situation. Much of what has already been said in the sections on the Group Cognitive Map and on Group Roles and Member Skills points to the requirements for an effective democratically oriented discussion group. A group must have some notion of how it should operate, some standard of performance, or, in our terms, a list of criteria. The criteria function as a goal and also as a standard against which to measure current performance.

A list of criteria is presented here which is not by any means exhaustive, but is intended to cover the major conditions that are required for the efficient operation of the *LTD* method. All groups should be encouraged to add to this list as their experience dictates. The criteria are presented here in tabular form, and then each is discussed in detail.

LIST OF CRITERIA

1. Prevalence of a warm, accepting, nonthreatening group climate.
2. Learning is approached as a cooperative enterprise.
3. Learning is accepted as the raison d'être of the group.
4. Everyone participates and interacts.
5. Leadership functions are distributed.
6. Group sessions and the learning task are enjoyable.
7. The material is adequately and efficiently covered.
8. Evaluation is accepted as an integral part of the group operation.
9. Members attend regularly and come prepared.

1. *Prevalence of a warm, accepting, nonthreatening group climate.* In the last few years there has been an impressive number of studies reported in education literature attesting to the value for learning of nonthreatening classroom environment. A climate of acceptance is an important factor in any learning situation. It is of particular importance in the *LTD* method, which requires a student to expose his ignorance,

confront his fellow students and in other ways dissolve his interpersonal defenses. This kind of behavior will be attempted only in a warm and accepting climate. Most of the points made in the ensuing criteria assume the operation of such a group climate.

2. *Learning is approached as a cooperative enterprise.* Students reared in the traditional academic manner unconsciously accept the idea that the competitive orientation is the *only* way to succeed. Aggressiveness, one-upmanship, attempts to impress, status seeking, and competitive behavior are seen as dysfunctional in the *LTD* method. For instance, many students have come to believe that if they have nothing brilliant or witty to say, they had better remain silent, and they usually do. Rewards and approbation must be given to cooperative behavior. The learner, not the learned, is the good group member. Asking for help in understanding promotes understanding for all.

3. *Learning is accepted as the raison d'être of the group.* The point of having a discussion group is to promote learning. This is obvious, but in a cohesive group it can become obscured. In some groups, members may become so enamored with the cohesiveness of the group that the goals of the group may become obscured. Because of the relative rarity in our society of satisfactory group experiences, there will be a tendency for members to use such an opportunity, when it does arise, unduly, to satisfy legitimate interpersonal needs.

4. *Everyone participates and interacts.* A group in which only a few members participate is obviously not a good group. On the other hand, it is not possible to have participation meted out into absolutely equal shares. Nevertheless, all members should participate some of the time. If a member does not participate, he may not be getting much from the group; but what

is more important, he certainly isn't contributing anything to the group. When silent members are questioned about their lack of participation, they characteristically respond, with a note of virtue in their voices, that while they may not be participating, they are getting a lot out of the discussion, and that they remain silent so that the better informed members can give the group the benefit of their wisdom. The *LTD* method needs for its successful operation the contribution of *all* group members and particularly of those who do not fully comprehend. If we hear only from those who 'know,' then it would be more efficient to get 'the word' from the instructor in the first place.

By interaction is meant the reacting of members to each other. Participation is differentiated from interaction, even though interaction is dependent on participation, because it is possible to have high participation and low interaction concurrently. For example, in groups where each member takes his turn in reciting from the assignment, there is little attention paid to the current speaker since his audience is not listening, but silently rehearsing. If there is little interaction, there is also little learning.

5. *Leadership functions are distributed.* Responsibility for making the group operate should not be delegated to or usurped by one or a few members. The Group Roles discussed in the previous section must be performed in order for the group to function adequately and for learning to take place. If all the members are going to learn, they must all participate, interact, and perform leadership functions.

6. *Group sessions and the learning task are enjoyable.* While mottoes like 'learning can be fun' repel the sophisticated reader, something needs to be said on the subject since this rather detailed analysis of discussion groups may have suggested to the reader that a group is to perform in a very serious fashion. Group discussion is not meant to be a grim business. Quite the contrary! Some frustration will inevitably be encountered in the

beginning, but the result intended is for learning to become re-warding, satisfying, and even exciting. When the members are grimly and methodically trying to learn, something is wrong with the operation, and evaluation of the process is in order.

7. *The material is adequately and efficiently covered.* The significance of this point for learning is self-evident and well labored in the section on the Group Cognitive Map.

8. *Evaluation is accepted as an integral part of the group operation.* A good group is one that accepts the inevitability of encountering problems and is willing to evaluate its progress. Perhaps enough has been said on evaluation, but even with groups that fully accept the foregoing statements this step is frequently bypassed. The reason for this bit of cognitive disso-nance is that a group gets caught in a vicious circle. If all goes well in a group, there is time for evaluation, but little need for it. If the group gets into difficulties, it needs evaluation, but, seemingly, has little time for it, because the problem itself is time consuming. In short, the paradox is that when a group has no time for evaluation, it probably needs it most. The instructor must insist on group evaluation.

9. *Members attend regularly and come prepared.* Any small group is demoralized and rendered ineffective by the irregular attendance of group members. Besides problems of continuity, the members who do come secretly feel foolish and resentful at being party to what is apparently considered by some as not worth the effort. If members come unprepared, the *LTD* method absolutely will *not* work. Unprepared members can get something out of attending, but they are parasitic to the life of the group. Also they can be quite detrimental if they insist in bluffing their way through. There must be a group standard that members attend regularly and come prepared. If the latter standard is not met, there should be an auxillary standard re-quiring the unprepared members to keep quiet.

HOW TO MAKE
LTD WORK

MANY STATEMENTS have been made throughout the text on the roles and responsibilities of the instructor and the members. The foregoing remarks can be summarized by saying that both the instructor and the student are responsible for behaving in ways that will hold the group to the Group Cognitive Map and will fulfill the Group Roles and meet the List of Criteria. In this section we will not repeat what was previously said, but will attempt to place the instructor and the members in their proper relationship to the *LTD* method.

Role of the Instructor

There are two roles the instructor plays in the group. One concerns subject matter and the other group performance. These will be taken up in order.

The quality of learning is obviously limited by the quality of the materials used in the course. As in any course, the instructor must select carefully the text or readings. It sometimes happens that the instructor feels that there is no adequate text in the field, and he must therefore cover the subject through his lectures. In such instances he should write out his lectures. duplicate them, and make them available in advance to the class.

During class periods, one role the instructor assumes is technically called resource expert. In this role he should not rescue the group every time they encounter difficulty, if they are to learn to think for themselves. There are occasions, however, when they do not have the background to resolve their confusion, and the text is not of much help. On these occasions the group should call on the resource expert. This task is more difficult to perform in large classes which are broken down into several small discussion groups.

Usually he will circulate from group to group and be available if needed. Another technique is to hold meetings of the entire class once a week and answer questions that have originated in the small group discussions.

Another role that the instructor plays in the class is technically termed group trainer. Because of the students' lack of familiarity with learning in discussion groups and with the *LTD* method, the instructor must do some training of the members of his class. The first item of business is to acquaint the students with the mechanics of the Group Cognitive Map, the Group Roles and Member Skills, and the List of Criteria. This manual, hopefully, will lessen the burden, particularly if each member has a copy.

Once the group is launched, the training role alters and also becomes fused with the resource expert role. As the meetings are to be conducted democratically, the instructor should participate minimally. His main job is to observe how the group is progressing with the *LTD* method. He then feeds back his observations to the group and may offer suggestions for overcoming difficulties that the members have encountered. In large classes some variation has to be made. Visiting the small groups, noting their difficulties, and then reporting the observations to the reassembled total group has worked in practice. Another variation is for each small group to appoint its own process observer to make notes on the group operation, while abstaining from the discussion. The process observers then make brief reports to the total group. The fact that each of the small groups discusses the same material and has approximately the same difficulties results in the report from a process observer being of value to all the class. This technique of course does not preclude observations and interpretations on the part of the instructor. A byproduct of this technique is the value that the process observer derives from the experience. He usually gets a much clearer perspective of the *LTD* method than any amount of instruction could provide. If this technique is employed, it is suggested that the process observer role be rotated among the group members.

An instructor should approach the training job creatively. He should devise his own variations of the method and experiment with different approaches in order to improve it. Variations have been tried, and a number of tricks of the trade have been evolved. Some of these techniques are adaptations made by previous instructors and may be of some help to prospective ones.

1. In introducing a class to the method, it is usual to give a brief explanation of the need for structure in group discussion and explain the three elements of *LTD* (Group Cognitive Map, Group and Member Roles, and List of Criteria) and how they aid in solving problems inherent in group discussion. Such a classroom presentation has been video taped and is available from the author. This presentation is on casette, in color, has a sound track, and runs thirty minutes. Also, in our mode of operation it is required that all participants acquire a copy of this book and read it prior to the first discussion session.

2. Conduct a demonstration group in which the instructor assumes responsibility for moving the group through the *LTD* steps.

3. Designate a leader from the group who will assume responsibility for getting the group to follow the *LTD*

method. His job would be procedural rather than didactic. As in the case of the process observer, a designated leader learns a great deal about the operation of the method and usually becomes a better group member. Consequently, this duty should be rotated so that all members have the opportunity to be designated leaders. This has been found to be quite successful in activating nonparticipating members. When the *LTD* method is fairly well assimilated there should be no need for a designated leader.

4. In preparing for the discussion, the student is required to make out preparation sheets. These will be discussed in the immediately following subsection. In aiding and reinforcing this operation, the instructor might make out a model preparation sheet and circulate it as a guide. Or he might have them handed in and corrected and returned. Also, the preparation sheets could be graded and contribute to the determination of the student's final grade in the class. When a level of proficiency has been obtained for the preparation sheets, grades could be assigned on the basis of class contribution.

5. Initial meetings might deal with easier material, and the group could practice on subject matter that was not of crucial importance.

6. Experience suggests a ground rule by which the group members are not to open their texts during the discussion, although they may make references to the preparation sheets. Otherwise, students bury themselves in the text, and interaction suffers drastically. It could be permissable to consult the text only for points of fact.

7. The list of Group Roles can be converted into a rating sheet, and the members can rate themselves, each other, or the group, as to the frequency with which various roles are performed. Just the act of filling out the rating sheet may sensitize members to weaknesses in their own performance. In large classes composed of several subgroups, having these filled out from time to time may provide the instructor with some

check on the groups. Similarly, some sort of postmeeting reaction sheet on which the students check or otherwise indicate their reactions and evaluations of the group meetings can be useful (see appendix).

Usually we have the members fill out the postmeeting reaction sheets before we begin our Step Nine discussion. Also, we ask the designated leader to tally the postmeeting reaction sheet responses and feed them back to the group, indicating the percentage of responses in each category. When these are accumulated, so that the group can see how the ratings have shifted over a span of several meetings, this often leads to some insightful discussions of the group and its problems.

One final word to the instructor. The *LTD* method will work only if the instructor is firm in his demand that the group follow the method.

Role of the Student

Very simply restated, the role of the student in the *LTD* method requires that he internalize and implement the Group Cognitive Map and that he play most of the group roles and that he tries to make his behavior consistent with the criteria. In particular, there are five interaction behaviors which he should practice.

1. Restate in his own words what others have said.
2. Sponsor other members.
3. Give encouragement and approval.
4. Formulate and cite examples.
5. Ask questions.

Two matters have been postponed, which will be dealt with now. One concerns group evaluation, and the other deals with preparation.

In preparing for a discussion, as in all studying, the student should read the assignment over once to get the general sense of it. For the *LTD* method, he should then approach the article as if he were conducting a silent or fantasy group meeting and prepare contributions that he might make at each step of the cognitive map. A preparation outline is provided, and the kinds of information to be noted are indicated for each step which will be dealt with during the discussion.

OUTLINE FOR PREPARATION

Step 1 — *Definition of terms and concepts*
List all the words of which you are unsure. Look them up and write down the definitions of them.

Step 2 — *Statement of author's message*
Write down your version of a general statement of the author's message.

Step 3 — *Identification of major themes*
Identify the subtopics in the article.

Step 4 — *Allocation of time*
Note the subtopics which you had trouble comprehending or which you think would provide a profitable discussion.

Step 5 — *Discussion of major themes and subtopics*
Write out a brief statement of the subject matter of each subtopic. Design a question that you would ask for each.

Step 6 — *Integration of material with other knowledge*
Write down the meaning or usefulness the material has for understanding other concepts. Indicate

what other ideas the material substantiates, contradicts, or amplifies.

Step 7 — Application of the material
Write down how the material can apply to your own life situation—past, present or future, or what implications the article has for your own intellectual interests or pursuits.

Step 8 — Evaluation of author's presentation
Write down your reactions and evaluation of the assignment.

If the student complies with the above preparation outline, he has learned a great deal before the discussion begins. As the discussion goes along, he might include additional ideas he has garnered. The outline then becomes an excellent source of review for examinations.

If everyone prepares in accordance with the outline above, the discussion can move along with remarkable ease and efficiency. When the designated leader inquires, for example, what the author's message is, the members need not go into shock, or start frantically looking through the article, or even busy themselves trying to think up an answer. All they need do is share with the group what they have recorded on their preparation sheets. And so it goes for all the steps of the Group Cognitive Map.

In our experience, we have found it particularly effective to have the preparation sheets handed in at the end of each class session. The instructor evaluates them and makes suitable marginal notes before returning them at the next session. This feedback enables the student to improve on his preparation sheets seriously. In courses where grades are required, part of the grade can be based on the preparation sheets, as well as on class participation and examination performance.

In diagnosing deficiencies and difficulties in the group operation itself, the member should assess what is going on by asking himself three questions.

1. Are we following the Group Cognitive Map?
2. Are there any missing Group Roles?
3. Are any of the criteria not being met?

The answers to these three questions should pinpoint the trouble that the group is experiencing—and the remedy.

On the basis of our experience, and that of our colleagues, we present a list of skills and techniques that individual members should practice to facilitate discussion.

SKILLS USEFUL FOR CLASSROOM DISCUSSION

Before the Discussion

Preparation

a. Start your preparation with a copy of the discussion outline before you.

b. As you read, jot down ideas wherever you think they fit best into the discussion.

c. Look up and learn to say the meanings of new words and concepts.

d. When you have finished reading, go back through the outline and write down reminders of what you might say during each step in the discussion.

e. Practice saying or formulating questions about material you anticipate introducing into the discussion.

During the Discussion

Step 1 — Definition of terms and concepts

a. List the words or concepts with which you had some difficulty and ask others to add to your list.

b. Try to define or explain one of the words on your list.

    c.   Ask the group members if you have defined it as they understand it.

    d.   Encourage others to practice explaining what it means to them.

    e.   Restate what someone else has said to make sure you understand it.

    f.   Give an example to clarify the meaning.

    g.   Ask someone else in the group to give an example.

    h.   Ask the group members if everyone understands the new words or concepts.

Step 2 — Statement of the author's message

    a.   State in your own words what you think the assignment was all about.

    b.   Frame a question that will encourage someone else to state what the assignment was about.

    c.   Encourage other group members to practice explaining it.

    d.   Add to what someone else has said.

    e.   State the ways in which your understanding or interpretation differs from that stated by another member.

    f.   Ask for clarification on points you don't understand.

    g.   Restate what someone else has said if you need to, to be sure you know it.

    h.   If you think two other members are misunderstanding each other, try to lessen the confusion.

Step 3 — Identification of major themes

    a.   Note organization of author's material in terms of headings and subheadings used.

    b.   Consider what makes for a logical sequence of subtopics.

    c.   Write on blackboard, so that all can see the suggested subtopics. This speeds the process and reduces confusion regarding what subtopics are proposed.

Step 4 — Allocation of time

a. Consider which topics are the most and least difficult to comprehend.

b. For each subtopic, formulate a question that would initiate a profitable discussion.

c. Calculate total time remaining and subtract estimated time allocated to steps 6, 7, 8, and 9. This gives time remaining to be distributed among the subtopics.

d. Do time allocation on blackboard so that all may see what they are agreeing to.

e. Appoint a timekeeper. Instruct him to announce when the group has two minutes remaining for discussion of a section.

Step 5 — Discussion of major themes and subtopics

a. Ask the group to state the essential elements of the author's presentation, e.g.:

  1. Hypotheses
  2. Methods
  3. Devices
  4. Techniques
  5. Arguments
  6. Sources

b. Practice saying for yourself what the author was mainly concerned with and encourage others to do so.

Step 6 — Integration of material with other knowledge

a. State the meaning or usefulness of the new material in understanding other ideas or concepts.

b. Phrase questions to put to the group members which will stimulate them to see how the new material fits into what they have studied previously.

    c.   Ask or state how the new material contradicts, substantiates, or amplifies some previously developed point.

    d.   Summarize into compact statements points others have made.

    e.   Listen critically for and try to state puzzling aspects of the material that are giving the group trouble.

    f.   Ask for or give help in stating the material more concisely.

    g.   Ask another member to restate what he has said if you think you may have misunderstood, or restate what you heard in your own words to ask for clarification.

    h.   Call the group's attention to and reinforce a comment that seems particularly helpful.

Step 7 — Application of the material

    a.   Ask or state why and how the new material can be useful to members.

    b.   Give examples of how you might apply it or how the knowledge of it may be useful to you.

    c.   Compare to your own experience the author's reasons for thinking it worthwhile.

    d.   Test the usefulness of the new material by constructing a situation for which it should be useful.

    e.   Give examples you know of which the new material helps to explain or helps you to understand.

Step 8 — Evaluation of author's presentation

    a.   State questions to help the group evaluate the new material, the method of arriving at the conclusions, etc.

    b.   State points supporting or questioning the validity of the arguments or the reasoning of the author.

    c.   State why and how you think the new material is or is not useful.

    d.   Frame questions which will help the group to test the usefulness of specific points.

OPTIMIZING THE LTD RESEARCH AND EVALUATION

THE *LTD* **HAS BEEN USED** all over the country by a great many instructors in a great variety of courses. The author has used it successfully in courses in psychology, sociology, statistics, research methodology, and public administration in a large number of universities. It has also been used in training probation officers in twenty-five counties in California, and in Nevada and Jamaica. In addition, we have in our files many unsolicited letters from instructors reporting success and satisfaction with the *LTD* method.

All the above testimonials and the self-claims of the author are not likely to impress anyone who is skeptical of the discussion method in general or of the *LTD* in particular. Hopefully a better case can be made in the research reports that follow. In our research efforts, we believe we have developed some ways to optimize the use of the *LTD*.

The first major effort to demonstrate the effectiveness of the *LTD* was conducted by the author at Idaho State University. The author and Dr. Shanna McGee each taught a section of introductory psychology, the former using *LTD* and the latter lecturing. In the following quarter, the study was replicated, but the roles were reversed: Dr. McGee used the *LTD*, and the author lectured. The same multiple-choice objective questions were used in all four classes, with two exams during the quarter, plus a final examination. The findings for this study were consistent with that of others comparing discussion and lecture, in that there was no significant difference in grades obtained between the two types of instruction regardless of which instructor used discussion or lecture. Two things might be pointed out, however. First, Bloom (1954) in his study of lecture versus discussion, found that objective factual recall favored the lecture method, whereas discussion had greater impact on subjective manipulative processes. Thus, the criterion worked against the discussion method in this study. Second, it is worth noting that the trend analysis was suggestive. In the first test, the students in the lecture were superior to the discussion students. In the second test, they were, on the average, about the same. On the final exam, the *LTD*-instructed students were superior, albeit not significantly so. It has been found also that most students exposed to *LTD* report on their *LTD* Evaluation Forms (Appendix) that they would use the method if they were ever to teach a similar course.

In our large study of the training of probation officers in group counseling (Hill, Stoller, and Straub 1967) more than thirty of our trainees became instructors in their agencies and trained other probation officers using the *LTD* method.

A study was conducted by Gutzmer (Gutzmer and Hill, 1973) on a University of Utah class in graduate education which employed *LTD*. Members were required to fill out Post Meeting Reaction Sheets (Appendix) after each meeting, and the class sessions were rated on a form designed to measure the quality of interaction in small groups, the Hill Interaction Matrix, Form HIM-G (Hill, 1969). The members' satisfaction with the class discussions as rated on the PMRs showed that, on the average, a high level of satisfaction was reported from the outset and in the final meetings there were unanimous ratings of excellent. Also the HIM-G ratings were good from the outset, but indicated steadily increasing and more consistent high quality interaction in the final meetings.

In a study conducted by Downs (1972), a number of classes conducted by different instructors at California State Polytechnic University—Pomona were involved in using the *LTD*, and the students were required to evaluate their experience on the *LTD* Evaluation Form (Appendix). Analysis of these data indicated that a very high proportion of the students rated the *LTD* experience as very good or excellent overall, and only a small minority rated it as a negative experience. While this was gratifying, some variations in the satisfaction levels were nonetheless revealing. Overall, some instructors got higher ratings than others and for any given instructor there was variation from class to class or course to course. In addition considerable variation was found in the average satisfaction score between discussion subgroups within the same class. In this investigation, the Hill Interaction Matrix Form HIM-B (Hill, 1969) was administered at the outset. Only a total score was used, called the Total Acceptance Score (TAS), and is considered as an index of how receptive students might be to discussion groups. It was found that the groups with high average TAS scores tended to have high satisfaction scores and those having low average TAS scores had lower satisfaction ratings. This can be interpreted as indicating that the group composition factor may be affecting satisfaction with *LTD*.

From this study, it was concluded that, while there was overall satisfaction with the method by the participants, nonetheless there were indications that (a) subject matter, (b) instructor, and (c) group composition may be acting in some way to decrease the satisfaction of students with *LTD* discussion groups.

As a consequence, an Innovation in the Instructional Process grant was obtained from the Chancellor's Office of the California State Universities to optimize the *LTD* method. The presentation below of the study is condensed, oversimplified, and selective. (The comprehensive report has not as yet been completed by the author.)

(1) The more technical the text, the less satisfaction was expressed with the *LTD* experience. The texts in engineering and the transformational grammar in English were associated with lower satisfaction scores as derived from the *LTD* Evaluation Form. Educators have long claimed that the single most important act of the instructor lies in the selection of the text. This is crucially important in the *LTD* method.

(2) The HIM-B scores of the engineering students were much lower than those of the humanities and social science students. This is interpreted as meaning they were less open to and sophisticated about small group situations. Their ratings on the PMRs of the group meetings were lower, and as was their satis-

faction with the *LTD* experience as rated on the *LTD* Evaluation Form. The lower ratings were not disastrous, and the instructors felt that with a more appropriate text and with beginning engineering students, the method had much promise.

(3) For certain courses in the study, group composition was experimentally varied, and members were placed in discussion groups according to their HIM-B scores. Five different types of groups were thus composed:

a.   All members had high TAS scores.

b.   All members had medium TAS scores.

c.   All members had low TAS scores.

d.   Group had high, medium and low TAS scores.

e.   Group had medium and low TAS scores.

The results obtained are very clear. The high TAS groups were high in their PMR and the evaluation scores, and the low TAS groups were low for both scores. Thus, to optimize the *LTD* it is only necessary to exclude the students who have a traumatized approach to group situations and a presumed reluctance to participate. This is, of course, not ordinarily possible, and the instructor has to teach the students who enroll in his or her class. It is very significant, therefore, to note that both the low and the medium and low groups (c and e) do less well, but the group that has high, medium, and low does quite well. This means that if the instructor can avoid having *all* low and medium students in the discussion groups and have *some* high TAS types in each group, a highly satisfactory result can be anticipated.

REFERENCES

Bloom, Benjamin. The thought process of students in discussion. In, Accent On Teaching, Ed. Sidney J. French, Harper, New York, 1954.

Downs, Patricia. Study of discussion groups. Unpublished Senior Project, California State Polytechnic University, Pomona, 1972.

Gutzmer, W. H. and Hill, Wm. F. Evaluation of the effectiveness of the Learning Thru Discussion method. Small Group Behavior, 4, 1, 1973.

Hill, Wm. F., Stoller, F. H., and Straub, Constance. Group therapy for social impact. American Behavioral Scientist, XI, 1, 1967.

Hill, Wm. F. Hill Interaction Matrix (HIM) Supplement, Claremont, California, 1969.

APPENDIX

POSTMEETING REACTION SHEETS

(PMRS)

I. REACTIONS TO GROUP MEETING

Name:_____

Date:_____

Instructions: Mark an X on the line above your response to the following questions.

1. I felt that the group meeting today was:

| Excellent | Good | Average | Not So Good | Bad |

2. I felt that my participation in the group was:

| Very Good | Good | Average | Not Very Good | Bad |

3. My feelings during the meeting were mainly:

| Very Enjoyable | Pleasant | So-So | Unpleasant | Quite Unpleasant |

4. I felt that I learned from the discussion:

| Very Much | Quite a Bit | Some | Little | Not at All |

Remarks:

II. EXECUTION OF COGNITIVE MAP

Instructions: For each of the eight steps of the Cognitive Map, indicate your rating of how the group performed the step by placing a check mark in one of the five boxes.

RATINGS

Steps in the Cognitive Map	1 Very Good	2 Quite Adequate	3 Fairly Good	4 Not So Good	5 Poorly
1. Definition of Terms					
2. General Statement					
3. Subtopics Designation					
4. Time Allocation					
5. Subtopic Discussion					
6. Integration					
7. Application					
8. Evaluation					

III. MEMBER ROLES INVENTORY

Instructions: Please check which of the following roles you played some of the time today by making check marks in the A column opposite the roles you played.

Please check which of the following roles you felt were exercised adequately by the group today by making check marks in the B column opposite those roles which were played.

Positive Roles

A	B		A	B	
__	__	Initiating	__	__	Gave examples
__	__	Gave information	__	__	Asked for examples
__	__	Asked for information	__	__	Gave clarification, synthesis or summary
__	__	Gave positive reactions or opinions	__	__	Asked for clarification, synthesis or summary
__	__	Gave negative reactions or opinions	__	__	Gave comment on group's movement or lack of it
__	__	Asked for positive reactions or opinions	__	__	Asked for comment on group's movement or lack of it
__	__	Asked for negative reactions or opinions	__	__	Sponsored, encouraged, helped, or rewarded others
__	__	Gave confrontation or reality tested	__	__	Standard setting
__	__	Gave restatement of others' contributions	__	__	Physical movement of objects
__	__	Asked for restatement of others' contributions	__	__	Relieved group tension

Negative Roles

A	B		A	B	
__	__	Acted with aggressiveness and hostility	__	__	Sought sympathy
__	__	Made self-confessions	__	__	Pleaded for a pet idea
__	__	Acted with defensiveness	__	__	Horsed around
__	__	Was competitive	__	__	Was dominating
__	__	Withdrew	__	__	Did some status seeking

CALIFORNIA STATE POLYTECHNIC UNIVERSITY, POMONA
LTD EVALUATION FORM

Name _____

Class _____

Instructor _____

Subgroup _____

You are being asked to complete this questionnaire in order to evaluate systematically the Learning Thru Discussion method. Your evaluation will be kept confidential so that your instructor will not be able to identify individual responses.

Please circle the response that most closely reflects your feelings.

1. Was this your first experience in a discussion group class?
   a. yes   b. no

2. Have you previously had a course using the LTD method?
   a. yes   b. no

3. What was your initial reaction to the LTD method?
   a. enthusiastic   d. slightly negative
   b. sounded o.k.   e. negative
   c. wait and see

4. Were you aware that the LTD method was to be used when you signed up for the class?
   a. yes   b. no

5. Do you feel that the method used was appropriate for the subject matter?
   a. yes   c. no
   b. partly

6. Do you feel that the instructor adequately supported and implemented the LTD method?
   a. yes   b. no

7. How much time did the instructor sit in your discussion group?
   a. not at all   d. frequent visits contributing
   b. very little   meaningfully to the group
   c. occasional visits   discussion

8. What determined your grade?
   a. tests
   b. peer evaluation
   c. preparation sheets
   d. a combination of a, b and c (specify)

9. In your experience has the LTD method been useful in the mastery of material that otherwise would have been difficult?
   a. yes
   b. no

10. Do you feel that you ended up with a real understanding of the basic facts of what the author had to say on the subject?
   a. yes
   b. partly
   c. no

11. In your opinion did the group cognitive map lessen the amount of time spent in useless argument?
   a. yes
   b. no

12. Was the definition of terms and concepts helpful in group communication?
   a. yes
   b. somewhat
   c. no

13. Did your discussion group relate itself according to the time limit set by the group?
   a. yes
   b. sometimes
   c. no

14. Do you think your ability to think critically was enhanced by the LTD method?
   a. yes
   b. somewhat
   c. no

15. In your group was there a prevalence of a warm, accepting nonthreatening climate?
   a. yes
   b. no

16. Did you feel you were competitive towards other members?
   a. yes
   b. no

17. Would you rate the level of interaction in your group as:
   a. high
   b. medium
   c. low

18. Were the leadership functions adequately distributed?
   a. yes
   b. no

19. In your opinion, were the members effective as group leaders?
    a. yes   b. no

20. Did the group session make the learning task more enjoyable for you?
    a. yes   b. no

21. Was the subject matter in the book adequately and efficiently covered?
    a. yes   b. no

22. How many members did not attend regularly?
    a. everyone   d. a few
    b. nearly everyone   e. practically none
    c. about half

23. How many members usually did not come prepared?
    a. everyone   d. a few
    b. nearly everyone   e. practically none
    c. about half

24. Do you feel that your participation in the method has changed the way you feel about other people?
    a. yes   c. no
    b. somewhat

25. Do you feel that your participation has changed the way you feel about yourself?
    a. yes   c. no
    b. somewhat

26. If the occasion should arise, would you ever use the LTD method in teaching or administration?
    a. yes   b. no

Discussion Questions

A. Are there any ways in which you would like to see the LTD method changed? If so do you have any suggestions for alternatives?

B. What do you see as the major advantages of the discussion method as compared to the lecture method?